Hustle Poet

The Beginning

Vol. I

Amaarah Gray

AMAARAH GRAY
PUBLISHING

Hustle.

Create.

Align.

Win.

Xo.
A. Gray

Ratchet.

1

Ratchet

I argued with God today.
Yes, I had a bit of a cry.
A moment in the sun filled with a plethora of why.

I argued with the I Am.
It's not something I'm proud of.
Someone had to check the Almighty,
Don't act like this is something unheard of.

A daughter/father come to Jesus moment,
A firm talking to of "what the hell are you doing?"
A stern discussion of frustration He pushed me to.
A bitter coffee,
An Irish wish espresso with no chaser.
That's what this word was brewing.

I demanded answers.
Pigtails in complete disarray.
I needed answers that turned into thesis statements,
Anything that was gonna settle this nagging feeling.
Truly,
This is so not okay.
I was angered with my Father.
The El Shaddai,
The Yahweh,
The Adonai,
The Almighty Jah.

I learned a lot about perspective,
It's a bitch-
That much I will say.

Hustle Poet

It isn't every day I wake up grateful of an act that can
condemn souls to a more permanently heated stay.

I needed clarity.
The robbed essence of my best friend Ashley.
I needed conclusions,
Essays,
Descriptive acknowledgment of fuckery unsettling.
Responses garnered to explain the state of the world,
I mean truly-
Where the hell was He in all his glory?

Did he go on holiday?
A shopping excursion in Hawaii,
A Hula of unstated fury.
A last minute trip filled with fishing.
If He ain't been up yonder-
I need to know whose ass I've been kissing.

I desired to know where He's been in summer.
I'm not sorry, God-
Time to disturb your peaceful slumber.

I banged on His cathedral doors,
I demanded educated retorts of grandeur.
I'm telling you the truth, Dolls.
On my Father,
This truth I'd never slander.

I marched right up to His desk,
Purse and gloves in hand.

I fixed my lipstick properly before tapping his shoulder
with my hand.

I gathered the boldness I stored in my heart,
A girl can't just use all of her charms on one excursion to
start.
I said, "excuse me, Mr. Almighty."
I did us proud, y'all.
Southern Wasp at it's finest.
I captured His complete attention,
On God y'all-
I was wildin'.

The Angels gasped,
The Seraphim whispered,
It was a scene of scandal to be noted in the Halos trilogy.
"What have you done to help our world, good sir? We are
damn near strung up in world war 3."

He was taken back,
His hand clutched to His chest was the tell tale turn of key.
He muttered, "who the fuck are you to question me?"

I answered:
Bold as fuck with a hint of snatched ratchet,
Rolling my neck to make sure He knew who he was talking
to,
"I'm 100% the one you made in your image."

And, that's what did it.
I made God laugh.

Hustle Poet

It's not an overrated experience.
I recommend it-
If you get the chance.

I needed to know why we live in a place where hate exists,
Why people dislike another without knowing where their
heart lies,
Why He could allow us to repeat the cycle of Sodom and
Gomorrah wrapped in apocalyptic political torture,
I had to know-
Did He no longer hear our cries?

"You're fucking up, God."
Yeah.
No fucks were issued.
Yeah, I said it.
Not my proudest moment for sure,
I'm positive at some point in the afterlife I'll regret it.

Truth be told-
I was on borrowed time,
No time to regret shit.
I had to say what I said,
I had to make sure the words hit
Or we won't be living to regret a future our ass can't miss.

I was so angry at God,
The sheer audacity of non-compliance.
The argument went round and round.
A hollering match perused.
Had St. Michael not intervened,

I would've had a hand full of white hair for sure.
He said, "my child, how do you know I'm not there for
sure?"

After much consideration,
I had St. Mike hold my beer.
I grabbed God by the hand,
walking with Him to show him proof of a world we can no
longer steer.

I showed Him how broken our people's spirits have
become,
The brokenness of the whole that persevered.
Pointed out that "thou shall not kill" thing people seem to
keep overlooking,
I showed him the evidence of God's children proud
pedophile men keep stealing, violating and selling.
I snitched on the lot of the heathens that pretend they
preach His word while they make money on Him,
False faith in droves they are dwelling.
I showed him the cries of innocence that go on mocked,
The "I can't breathe" screams,
The accusations of hate gained against one another.

Taking the opportunity,
I dared to ask once more.
God, is this really how we are supposed to be treating one
another?
Breonna Taylor,
Did you know she was planning to be a nurse to care for
others?
How can it be okay for them to kill an innocent 24-year-old

Hustle Poet

in her own home?
God, please bless her.
She could have been more than just someone's mother.
There's so many more than just her,
Michael, George, Trevon,
Just to name a few.
Then there's this whole thing with biased racism-
Sex preference,
Gay biased,
Even bias on women's rights of reproduction,
Insanity in so many forms.
Hate dressed up in one form of another,
It's like it's harder to accept love,
Easy to hate another,
To respect oneself completely.
How many more days we gon' live before you decide to
intercede?

He answered quite clearly,
Looked me in the eye to make sure I understood.

He exclaimed:
my child, I've been there with you,
Beside you,
Crying with you,
Watching as you witness the beatings.
A flex of free will is what's happening.
I have to wait for the people to fix themselves,
Inside is where the help is,
That's what everyone is needing.
I whispered my word into them at birth.

Ratchet

It's been there the whole time.
So don't sit here, whine and cry to the Divine.
I've done my job,
The task is yours now.
It's my time to unwind.
That's the answer to the truth you are seeking.
I've given you the world,
It's your turn to take the light.
It's now up to you to fix the world,
It's now up to you to stop this fight.
It's called earning your anointing,
That's the true definition of Heaven.
I've given you the rules to gain access.
It's up to you to live them.
They must take accountability,
They must remember whose child they exist in.
No cap,
That's what your world is needing.
Everyone is responsible for their own truth.
It's the people who need to fix their faith,
That's the choice the world is needing.
Stop questioning why,
really see who's words they are heeding.
It's them who has to fix what they deemed to undo.
Don't think it's me who has y'all cheating.

I simply created man.
It's now time for man to find their purpose,
Find a reason to make their life worth living.

And that's how it happened.

Hustlle Poet

God dropped the mic,
He walked away,
Slamming the door to His office.

I know I should have ran back in there-
I should have screamed,
"Where the hell is the justice?"

I had no choice.
My ratchet visit came to an end.
I had to leave Heaven if I ever wanted to make sure I still
exist.

I got us the answers.
The truth that we all seek to find.
They Didn't even validate my parking,
His angels are so rude when you simply want to have a
ratchet chat with the Almighty Divine.

Turns out we can't blame God for fucking this world up,
It's always been us who had the ability to fix it.
We are all more worried about stimulus packages,
Worrying about likes and social media tagging,
We remain so pressed about short term money to long term
problems,
We all forgot our home training.
We all forgot it's us who is killing us.
Acting like we are blind to the truth we see daily,
Don't blame God while crying out-
Does He think our world is worth saving?
It's time for us to fix our world.

Ratchet

It's time to grow the fuck up, y'all,
Stop playing.
It's time for us to change the times we live in,
It's the world your kids will live in,
START PRAYING.

Hustle Poet

My City.
I watch you . . .
All of you. . .
Rushing with angered intelligence;
Your children frustrated- fighting
like the demeaning words they enter matter
More when they register less;
Showing a lack of communication between
Generations. . .
Generations that remain enraged. . .
breathing in the Texas heat like the
Destined fired coals of shoal.
You're angered;
My city.
You wake to dreams that
For some reason-
Never become realized in a City that boasts
Cultural genius from every angle.
I watch you,
My city
And weep.
I cry for your lack of ambition,
Your mountains of know how.
I sob for the boldness of every beggar
Convalescing at every single stop light.
One dollar for an old soul.
An old soul who-
Perhaps knows how to savor misfortune but
Lounges on the scattered guilt of kindness and
Grand opportunity of the 3-second-stoplight.
My city...

Hustle Poet

Why beg when you are well and able to claim that
Possible dream you squander called life.
When did working for the abundance of a well-earned
meal,
A drink of distilled truth with no chaser,
The antiquated bite of an opportune apple
Become more shameful than begging for the
Earned fruits of another's labor?
My city.
So close to brilliance.
Innovative in cultural fusion.
We the People-
The Cultured;
The rhythmic
The few.
The promise of tomorrow is a loan of pawned expense.
How will you chase the scattered dawn of time?
My city.

Pretty Little Rotten Flower.

Pretty Little Rotten Flower
I'm the prettiest of the little willful rotten flowers.
Dowsing my creativity with flourishing doubt.
Trying to maintain the price of clout.
Hold your head up high.
Remember it's not whom you become.
It's who you are that demands presence, poise and fire.
Don't let the demand change your desire.
See we've come a long way...
Marching for rights and equal pay.
Voicing lyrical truths of modern concepts,
While the generations of now-
Drag the spice of cost and the cost of being earnest.
It's in between the way you carry a nation.
It's why Mya recognized the harmony in chosen words.
It's why she gave more than a voice to the cage bird that
sings.
It's more than the pretty women-
The ones who let value slip for vain fairytales Of drunk
ambition.
It's wrapped up in an ideal case of perspective.
Tribal, trivial and truth.

Pretty little rotten flower.
Who do you claim to be while your spirit shows you who
you are not?
Do you deem to lower your grace?
Twerk by twerk.
Bones and sockets that jerk.
Raise your standard.
Show the eavesdropping world the power of your story.

Hustle Poet

We survive in the details of pain.
We live to breathe the sorrows of a hurt, hushed whispers.
Don't speak knowing your words remain unheard.
It's more than just loins you gird.
Take power in realizing the unshakable truth...
Phenomenally flowered woman,
Guard each thought.
Bare each step.
More than just one sacred pretty little rotten flower.
It's the seeds you sow that will establish your power.

It's in the roots you lay.
It's in the way your spirit confronts the sun.
You have the ability to bend the wind.
You can't allow the greed in others to win.
You could rise in antiquated glory.
But, you allow caution to bend your ear instead?

Why play it safe when the world was built on challenges
and rise?
It's more than just a measured petal size.
Each step you dare to take.
If it's been paid for you by your ancestor's quake.
You wonder-
Do I have what it takes?
I am more.
I am simply too mistakenly great.
It's the words of importance.
That's what needs to be your drive.
That's what this thing has become.
It's this thing called life...

Pretty Little Rotten Flower

No need to rush.
You are more than just someone's wife.

Pretty little rotten flower.
Show the world there's more to life than simple thoughts
of anguish.
Don't showcase the abundance of strife.
Prettiest of the little rotten flowers.

Who's in your tribe?
Are they people that cause your spirit to run and hide?
Do they applaud when the days run into ruin,
Or shadow you just to learn what tea you've got brewing?
Are they your people who weep with you when you suffer?
A helping hand,
How hard is that for them to muster?
Do they cheer for you when your passion bleeds in sorrow?
If you left, would they still ride with you tomorrow?
These are things you need to consider,
Before you rise and celebrate with glitter,
Should you surround yourself with blood thirsty sharks,
If they cannot stomach the same road you walk?
You need to surround yourself with those who chase the
rise,
Who savor each word you dare to breathe,
Who show you-
You are wise.
You're the original lone wolf,
You're powerful on your own,
You don't need groupies,
Your practices are honed.
You need good tribesmen,
People who dare the day and storm with you into the night,
Who wouldn't second guess your loyalty, your passion,
your plight.
It's these type of people who are worth your thoughts and
your care,
It's those people who will show you-
They will always be there.
Learn how to spot a fraud,

Hustle Poet

When you identify the weakness within them
Simply say:
To you, evil do-er, be gone.
You have no more energy to give,
To those who can't brave the fight just like you did.
Why should you maintain their load another day,
It's always been you.
That's why they die another day to stay.
Show them why you're different, bold and too good,
You've learned all the lessons,
When you stood where they stood.
That's how you'll know,
Who remains worthy to be in your tribe.

Addiction.

Addiction

In the newness of you . . . I found your darkness.
It welcomed me immediately,
wrapped me tightly in its arms,
Caressing my conscious into nervous melodies of purple.
The immense Orchestra of pain existing within you-
That's the song I'm addicted to most.
It soothes my worries when my heart calls out for you
most.
You can't hear me.

In the newness of you,
I see who you truly are.
After the stigma melts away,
After the drugs dissipate the memory of who you once
were,
Inside crying to live a second of never could be. . .
After the old you stares out of the armor of fake you hide
behind.
I see you.
The intimate lover.
The exuberant lie.
It makes my soul hunger for another hit of almost.
I hear you.
Longing for me the way I once longed for the coldness of
your touch.
Burn me with your blue fire.
I'd beg-
Starving for the very thought of your raspberry colored
lips,
The words of fibs that will never live.
The taste of lost freedom.

Hustle Poet

I will always give you life,
I am the witness of your struggle,
Wrapped in the loneliness of a wife.

In the newness of you. . . I find who you were meant to be,
 Walking on the side of who I can never become.
I see you once more-
The boy hiding inside the man.
The comforter confronting the comforted.
Can you hear me, pretty bird?
You. . .
My blue colored marvel.
My bird without feet that sleeps in the hurricane winds of time.
I lay addicted to your song.

Why won't you let me hold you up while you attempt to land?
Do you burn the same blueness of tranquil fields?
Do you wonder how it is I can rewind the lapse of time?
I call to you.
I will always answer your beckoning bellow.
You ask how a heart like mine can still continue to beat.
Don't you see-
The choice has always been yours.
It's your song that burns within the walls of my chiming heart.

In the newness of you. . . You'll find a new start.
I will always love you completely,
My Blue Bird Addiction,
Even when you've ripped my beating heart.

Foot Race.

Foot Race

My eyes captured you,
The one my heart knew.
I've waited centuries to love you.
Miles of memories,
Lined up like a casket filled drive.
Lifetimes dreamt,
Filled with why nots and what ifs.
Moments checked for wonderful musings.
Did you ever consider me the same way?
What's the cost I'd pay to charm time to make our moment
last?

I'd die ten million deaths,
All in the name of living your myth.
I'd do anything to watch my name linger on your lips.
Whatever it took to earn your love.
Praying constantly to the sacrificial dove.

I'd collect moments of stolen glances,
Place them in my soul like decorated treasure.
Constant daydreams of considerable trysts.
Lost in the seconds I will always cherish,
Blessed by the pink hues of your insatiable lips.

Messy, tussled hair in your face.
The acceptance of disgraced love my heart would sing,
Soul renderings of unforgettable.
A pair of twins with your blue eyes and honey dipped
ringlets,
An ode to the day my soul bathed in the moonlight of you.

Hustle Poet

A black & white spotted dog named Moo,
The bark-filled mischief gussied up like the ruining of true
karma.
A clumsy Marmaduke with lanky legs,
The puppy God saved to make our world a better place.

The marathon we live,
Disguised as an uphill foot race. Momentum not ceasing.
Determined,
Motivated,
Unfuckwithable.
That's what it takes to deserve the masterpiece of you.
The courage of making myself into a success,
No matter what cause,
conflict or antiquated stress.

I'd do whatever it takes to secure the win,
The victory my heart cries out for.
Constant moving monument of my specified trophy.
That's the timeline we currently exist in.

The one continuous lap of unticked time.
Unsure if where the reason runs,
We do this in the one true name of the Divine.
The lapse of a could be,
The just kidding of an idea wrapped in the laugh of ha's
An earned excitement of what might be in store.
Eternity in a sharp blue suit.
Blue Balenciaga boots.
A gold Rolex.
The storyline of an intoxicating dream.

Foot Race

Acqua Di Gio mafia scented top notes,
A smile that would ruin me.
The essence of the one my soul adores.
Heaven dressed up like my naked truth.
That's what I see when I glance at you.
My future in a section of life not yet lived.
A constant living room performance of an off brand Les
Mis.

It's always been you.
The blue-eyed miracle.
You're more than a perhaps,
More than a destined meeting.
You're the one I've waited decades for,
The one my love never outgrew.

The answer to all inspiration.
A member of the infamous nation of Joey,
The source of pigmented sustainment in a world filled with
Gray glory.
Using my pain to tell every measure,
I'm the lady hero,
Never the damsel in any story.

If they seek, I will reveal.
I'd color their world in words that are coated with love to
heal,
I'd speak of the time it was when you stole my heart with
one look,
The diary of a woman completely shook.
The story of a celebrated portrait of a Hustle Poet.

Hustle Poet

A brisk painting of a pain destined to be feels.
You're the one hue my soul paints with,
The evidence of a realm that remains real.
Various shades of blush kissed true.
You're the one who captured me.
The color of blue my heart once knew.

32

Little Latin Girl.

Hustle Poet

Little Latin Girl,
So vibrant,
Skin of golden brown.
You roll your R's with heritage,
You're raised with tradition.
Stand up, girl
Be proud.

There is a reason you're different.
You're faith-based.
You're fiery.
Yes mama- it shows.

Your Mahogany eyes have seen triumph,
You've seen struggle when the progress slows.
You know what it's like,
To watch the magic to make ends meet.
You know how to make a 7-course meal,
To feed a blended family of 13.
Your cousins,
Your tias,
Even the local strays,
We've all become family.
Through tradition we pave the way.
You constantly deal with ignorance,
You'll eventually fight for equal pay.

Your heart sinks lower,
Day by day,
The people who scream go home,
As if it's their cause to say.

Hustle Poet

Why would they want you to return
to a street they've never crossed?
You'll wonder what would they do,
If it was them who had to bare what those people have lost.

No, you've never been out of country,
You're American,
Born and bred,
You'll learn from their example,
Never allow that thought of a person to enter your head.

Little Latin Girl,
Stay strong when you stop,
Stay silent and wonder,
Do they really know the cost?
Your family is made up of Veterans,
People you've had to live without,
People you've lost.
The ones you've shed tears for,
Night after night,
The brave men and women who went to fight.

When they say ignorant musings,
Don't sink to their disrespectful level,
Smile and nod at them kindly.

Remind them of your family's sacrifice,
The steps that gave them abilities,
the right to have free speech,
the right to sleep peacefully at night.

Little Latin Girl

Little Latin Girl,
Don't change when you watch the world become divided,
You are the future now,
Even if the ones who remain talking are severely blinded.

Grow up inspired,
Grow to be ambitious,
Work hard to make a difference,
Then come back running the place,
It'll be them who is left digging ditches.

Be strong,
Be wise.
Show them why the little Latin Girl they doubted,
Changed the world among their arrogant lies,
Right before their mouth started.

Evolution of Ego.

Evolution of Ego

I'm just a girl,
The first of my name,
Born into the land of plenty,
A mindset of whimsical,
A sparkle in the eyes of many.

I'm a learner of method truths,
A holy Roman Catholic Roller,
A sacrament holder,
A constant state of purity & youth.

I'm just a teenager,
A mindset of eyeshadow in electric blue,
An Ode to dancing in the dark with The Boss,
A statement of Aqua Net tresses,
Dressed to kill in Madonna Inspired dresses.

I'm a learner of hard knock guesses,
An 80's baby in glorious splendor.
My So-Called-Life is my guilty pleasure.
I'm more than just Tiger Beat,
Cosmo & YM Magazine Posters,
I'm a follower of Bon Jovi,
Aerosmith & the CRÜE that's too Motley.

I'm filled with inspiration considering what my future
might be.
I'm more than just Living On A Prayer.

I'm more than just halfway there,
I'm more than just 17.

Hustle Poet

I'm now just a U.S. Army Soldier.
I'm a mindset of duty, honor & service.

Following in the footsteps of family tradition,
College wasn't enough for a woman who was in transition.
I'm strong,
Courageous,
Brave,
Ambitious.

I'm a woman leading from the front,
That's now my true mission.
My life is hard now,
I know the hardship of being a soldier,
I'm flown many miles away in a day,
Surrounded by people I don't know.

It's crazy to consider the things I do now,
Just to earn a decent wage for pay.
I've learned the value,
lessons & the cost of war,
I've learned the effects our actions have on countries that
are now war torn.

I'm no longer a girl,
I'm just someone's wife.
There's so man moments I've collected now,
So many titles I've come to favor,
Girlfriend,
lover,
fiancée,

Evolution of Ego

Now I'm someone's mother.
I'm a mindset of boo boos & kisses that heal tears,
I'm a doggone superhero,
In one second-
My voice can scare away my baby's fears.

She's the apple of my eye,
Brown eyes & dimples with curls or plenty,
Now it's my turn to show her how a woman walks,
Rocking with poise & grace while strutting with #Fenty,
Looking back on life now,
I'm glad this is a marathon,
Not a race.

I've learned what loss feels like,
I've learned how to survive a broken heart,
I hope one day she'll understand why her father and I had
to part.
I'm more than just a woman now,
I'm an Idea,
A dream,
A reflection of a life well lived.

You can't tell beneath my smile,
I hide a lifetime of epic pain.
I've lived a life of struggle,
A life filled with strife.
I've made some colorful choices,
Living life on a prayer.

Hustle Poet

I now have a mindset of never give up,
A life of passion filled with purpose,
I'm a damn good woman,
In case you didn't know it.

 I'm more than the circumstances,
More than the shadows that tried to claim my life.
Don't let the flowery words fool you,
I'm in a damn good state of mind.

This Is the Evolution of a woman,
A constant trier,
A prize-winning fighter.

It's an Ode to my former self,
A glitter filled Venus of worship.
Next time you thank me for my service,
Remember - I started out just a girl with a dream,
A girl with an idea,
A girl with a purpose.

Hustle Poet

Naked.

Naked

I want to see you naked,
Take off the lies you wear as truth.
My eyes want to soak in the reasons behind your failure,
To understand you completely from the root.

I want to see you naked,
Take off your labels,
Dispel the true nature of your hidden inhibition.
Remove your knowing lack of definition,
In a quest for solving the equation within.

I want to see you naked,
It's a sought after sight to see,
My ears thirst for the clarity that teases your word filled
mind,
It's in the melody of your tales of woe,
I can hear the motive in your voice,
Apart of you,
I simply must be.

I want to see you naked,
Open the doors of your church,
Display your gospel,
Your word remains shook.
Let truth become your bible,
Your insight a holy hymn.
We will pray away the vanity,
We know the cost of sin.
I want to see you naked,
Shed the meekness hiding within,
I long to pray at your temple,

Hustle Poet

To caress my inspiration inside.
I see you in infinite wisdom,
Don't go against the tide.
I want to see you naked,
Drop the walls that surround your purpose,
Allow others to drink your pain,
Quench the thirst of onlookers,
Who now understand the price of fame.

I want to see you naked,
To absorb the darkness you keep company,
It's more than just my light you're addicted to,
In case you were wondering.
My eyes have now seen your nakedness,
I've sampled your constitution,
I've savored the fullness of your truth,
I now have full understanding,
I've witnessed the true version of you,
I've quenched my thirst on your blood shed.
I understand your labels,
your title is deceiving,
I am the light in the darkness
You've always been needing.

I see you completely naked,
My soul found what makes you inspired,
You've been created to be tough,
You absorbed the fire of what transpired,
I live to see you naked,
That's the gospel I now call proof,
I will always accept you,
No matter which lies you put on as truth.

Hustle Poet

The Swimmer.

The Swimmer

I drown when you reach for me.
Your water filled with liquid sin.
I struggle to breathe,
Gasping for truth while you choke on your lies.

Your touch.
It used to consume me.
I was filled with a world of want.
I wanted,
I savored the thought of being burned by you.
I considered it a flesh wound honor.
I'd watch the mischief in your eyes turn to darkened
cravings.
A thirst it was clear I'd never be able to quench.

I watch the now noticeable slip of anticipated shaking.
Words used to flow out of your soul like poisoned poetry.
I was enamored with the concept of you.
I'd consider the possibilities of old,
 Just to discover that you hale from opportunity of never
new.

I cling to life,
Bellowing to help you snap.
What they don't tell you is-
When you fall in love with a hidden junkie,
It's you who begins to snap.
It makes you old,
The tar in your veins,
Your black tar chains.
I spent hours wishing the world would stop you from your

Hustle Poet

chosen trade.

It's killing you.
Needle by needle,
In between your toes,
Pill by pill,
Dose by dose.

I've left you,
Well -what's left of you now.
I'm gaining confidence,
I'm breathing,
I've dealt with your lie-filled opinionated most.

What truth could a woman expect,
I've already combated the absence of your deathly host.
Time to face the facts,
So sad but true,
You never put the needle to my arm,
Never put the pill in my hand,
I was dying just the same with you,
I stood with you to be true.

Accepting your flaws,
Negating to stop your past time of choice,
Never to reprimand,
Beside you I would stand.

I've surfaced, my love,
The truth has set me free.
This is a cautionary tale,

The Swimmer

A reminder,
A notice.

The next time you see a woman drowning,
Don't just deem it okay to walk by,
Stand her up,
Clear her throat,
Get her to notice.

There's nothing beautiful about one-sided love that drowns,
Sometimes you have to save yourself,
No matter how bad it now sounds.

The Violin

The Violin

A twisted web,
We tangle,
We weave.
It's a tangled web of truths,
No one can handle the deceptive nature we perceive.
A tangle,
A tryst,
A misappropriation of proof.

A tangible reach for evidence,
Don't disregard the roost.
The lack of know how inspired,
Attach another angle,
No man remains a knight,
Pull tight another edge now,
Your flawed desire is now united.

Twisting,
Turning,
Connecting one strand to none,
A decorative conceptual reality,
The rapture has already begun.

Perverted corruption,
Spinning deep within.
Intertwined,
Inventive,
Don't mislabel your good deeds a sin.
Conjure conviction,
It's swelling,
Pulsating,

Hustle Poet

Threading deep within the surface.

A smirk so devious,
The sun bares witness to this midnight haunting.
The web,
So elegant,
So cunning in nature,
A well-balanced structure,
It won't spot the captured from yearning.

A superb casting,
The knotted enticing,
A glamorous failure of blue
A plan executed so well,
We will leave you withdrawing
from love twisted vices enthralling.

Come,
Little spider,
Accelerate your spindle,
Time waits for no one,
It's the fire within you that dwindles.

The Alter.

The Alter

I noticed her in the silent abyss.
She was always there watching,
Waiting for an opportunity to approach.
My nose wrinkled instinctively,
I didn't like her prose.

The way the words slipped off her tongue,
It was like poisonous ivy,
So quick to spread a rash,
So lethal I'd be struck down with envy.
She strutted when she stepped,
Each strike a calculated plan.

I searched for an avenue to avoid her,
Her energy was to suffocating to stand.
A sharp shutter pierced my being,
The moment she smirked a devilish grin.
I couldn't stomach being in front of her,
Every aspect of her was dripping perfection.
She was flawless,
So statuesque,
The endearing was an act-
I'm sure.
Infuriating,
So peppy,
This I surely cannot endure.

She spoke of positivity,
Smelling like all of Chanel's past obsessions.
I wondered what it would be like,
To be her just to secure the lessons.

Hustle Poet

Would I like being proper?

A ladylike costume for sure.
I wasn't sure I'd be able to stomach,
The faux accent she tried on while shopping.

You important, girl-
I'm sure.
My eyes seduced the time,
Begging for a few minutes to strike,
Did she not have anything better to do,
Like get lost or go fly a kite?

The moments scraped by-
Like they were doing my soul a favor,
Betty Crocker needed to kick rocks,
I could kill her and do the whole world a favor.

I'd make it look like an accident,
A heel broken in traffic-
So tragic,
Poetic at best
Or I could wait until she's showering,
A hairdryer connected by cord,
A slippery little sucker.
Electric paradise-
A score.

I could chop up her limbs in bite size pieces,
Feed her to my dog,
That might be a bit to messy,

The Alter

Might be better to be fed to the hogs.

I smirked silently into my reflection,
So pretty and pure,
Little did I know-
All I had to do to get her to leave,
Was tell my reflection
To stand up,
Then the Alter would be no more.

Praying.

Prying

My heart thought it knew yours in the shortness of time.
It paused to watch you breathe,
Basking in the ambiance of your glow.
Your heart was something I just had to know.

I was Intrusive,
I admit that,
I'll own it.
How could I know the pureness of your essence
When you refuse to show it.

I observed you from afar,
Stalking you like prey,
We'd be together someday.
This was fact,
No,
more like destiny I'd say.

I'd watch closely,
Memorizing every caress of your strong hands,
Until they hit her face,
We would now never be more like I had planned.
I sank to ground.
Hidden in a darkened corner,
I squeezed my head,
I cowered, shivered in terrifying shame.

How could my heart adore someone who fights ignorant
with his fists,
no matter the end result Or Pain?

I paused,
Conflicted,
I chose to fight back.

I grabbed a bar of rod iron,
Upon his head I did whack.

I prayed to God while shouting,
Forgive me, Lord;
This discord is a due justice.
My skin can't take another hit,
I'm sending him home to you,
Throw him deep into the pit.

I saved more than one woman that day,
I saved a million messes.
There's no telling who would have been at the end of his
bloody fists and rage,
At least now we won't have to confront it.
The next time your heart thinks it knows someone,
Tell It to turn a blind eye.

Put on your lipstick,
Place on your shades of the wise.
I could have been that girl,
I totally would have believed his lies.

I escaped by mistaken identity,
Be careful who your heart loves,
Next time there won't be an onlooker to save you like I
saved me in between the gushes.

My Immortal Beloved.

My Immortal Beloved

Beloved.
You move me.
Beyond measures I didn't think were achievable.
You move my spirit,
Renewing the pigmented colors of my Autumn colored sky.
You fill me.

My cup runneth more than just over.
You champion my cause,
When I have no flag to continue to fly in a windless sky.

You.
Beloved.
You leave me hungry,
Famished for the knowledge of your beating heart.
You leave my thirsting for the bellow in your laugh,
The rapturing blueness of the sparkle in your soul.

You feel me.
Even on the worst of days when the silence can't seem to
claim the whispers of my haunted mind.
You raise my chin,
When my mahogany eyes can't fathom just another glance,
You thrill me.
You find me in the battle of lost dreams.
You wake me up to a new level of determination,
Feverish,
Hoping,
Ambition filled.
I become the woman you recognize,
The "she" I cannot get my sight to see.

Hustle Poet

The Goddess Queen you paint portraits of,
Cherished by the soliloquies of your lullaby words.
You have resurrected the me who was dead inside.

You…
Beloved.
Have brought me back to life.
When the lovers who I've met in the world discarded my
soul amidst the wolves,
You've guided me.
Shielding me.
You gave me a home.
Your skillful hand reached out for mine
Like I was your saving Grace,
Broken-hearted,

You…
Beloved,
Believed in me.
When all I had to offer you was vapored hopes of once
more.
When my words fell of deaf ears.
You healed my wounds.
Bandaged my courage.
Helped me to embrace my freedom,
Claim my worth,

You…
Beloved.
You wrote your name in every lapsing breath that expels
from my person.

My Immortal Beloved

You became my north pointing star,
My protector,
My King.

You…
Beloved.
You embraced me.
As I am without expectation,
Without judgment,
Without need.

Grateful.
Me…
I am yours.
Beloved.

Word.

My life is made up of words,
Of melodic soliloquies,
Of ballads & tragic musings.
Words that paint poetry I find hidden,
in the moments of my highlighted history.

My life of words,
My symphony built of a collection,
My gift to a sleeping world,
My magnificent life's word Opus.

My words of vivid splendor,
The selected words to convey my truths,
Linger on the lips of many,
Inspiring a love kindled fire within,
Releasing the captured, tortured souls tragedy claimed
in the name of fictitious grandeur.

Deep in the painted syllables of love battles,
Some won,
Some lost.
My words,
My understanding of a toxic kissed world,
A dying society of reason,
Turning a blind eye to the loss of aided passion.
My words reignite the purpose of those dead inside.
Words,
Each giving meaning to explain the experience of being
seduced,
burnt by fire.
Foraged by true pain,

Hustle Poet

Molded by conviction.
It's my words that give intention permission to flourish.

My words.
Inspired as we speak truth into a poisonous existence,
The power in my words release thoughts in others that
become actions,
It's my words that encourage constant persistence in an
ambitious soul that remains sluggish.

My life of words,
It's how I was created.
God smiled and proclaimed,
"Ah, a Writer,
We'll turn her words into soldiers,
We will show the world her underestimated power."

My love of words,
It's deeply rooted.
My life is made up of words,
Of lullaby coated wind chimes.
My words will outlive me,
They are my legacy,
My swan song,
My impact,
My triumph.

I allow my words to move me,
To reveal my Earthly purpose,
I hope my words move your spirit,
So you'll learn the price a poetic life entails.

Like I Love You

Like I Love You

Like I love you,
I fell in love with you,
The way one falls in love with a violet sky.
Adoring you completely,
All at once.

I fell down a mountain,
Denying a truth of unholy war.
You stood beside the battlefield raging in me,
I love you-
Completely, Dear.
My darling.
My heart is yours,
Forever I'll be true.

The lies you sold me on,
Discounting my affection with a small amount of trying.
7 reasons for me to stay.
Each one impressing,
I realize now. . .
It was my soul you were compromising.
That was the day you shined in my eyes like a newly
minted copper penny.

Brown penny,
Brown penny.
Your shine was magnificently captivating,
Like a bee to the flowers your heart grew.
I was hooked to your thorns.
My soul called out to yours.
It was me who begged for your brand of blue.

Hustle Poet

Your voice had me hypnotized,
I followed you into the wild of the unknown,

Drinking every ounce of your holy water,
I'd wear the blame like a black Chantilly laced negligee.
I drank your liberty like it was the source of a fortified life.
I loved you . . . completely.

Your brokenness,
Every one of your causes.
Even when you were one helluva glorious disastrous
bastard.
I knew the idle talk about you,
The things others counted as tree filled truth,
The kind that is strong rooted,
Deserving,
I was the last to know,
One day you'd show me they were right 100 Proof.

I loved you, my darling,
The hurt in those words,
So poison-dipped but torturous & true.

They say you love the one who can't see the true you,
Facts like a love starved criminal.
I loved you-
My darling,
Even when I bowed to your heavy flaws.
It's taken 3 years now,
To set myself free from your sharpened claws.

The words "I love you, darling" now have a different

meaning.
It means I nod to the deadness within your spirit,
It's my heart you are no longer deceiving.
You're now a murderer,
You killed the man I loved beyond life itself,

Cutting him out with the harshness of words that formed
into the sharpness of a knife,
You killed the man who taught me how not to hate
someone who hates himself,
A man who will never be worthy of a love like mine,
A man with a broken heart who was never pure.

It's heartbreaking to watch you waste away to become a
stereotypical statistic,
All that promise and potential,
Shot up your vein,
Your life is circling the drain.
Can't you see yet?

I love you, my darling.
I love you, completely,
Even if it's your love I can no longer entertain like a
spoiled past expiration date.
One day you'll feel the loss when you surface,
By then you'll be claimed.

My love will remain with you until you expire,
Of that I'm sure,
You'll be one less punishment in this life,
I will stomach to endure.

In Transition

In Transition

I'm in transition.
A needed change.
A new start,
An adventurous journey,
To unbreak my heart.

I need difference,
The same way lungs need air.
I've learned so much about me in such a small time.
These facts which have always been present.
I learned how not give in,
I'm learning not to care.
I'm in transition.
It's amazing what one can learn,
When they aren't breathing toxic scents in,
When it's not you for which I yearn.
I wish I could go back to that day,
The day of understanding,
It would be more than just a recourse,
Out of your shadow I'd be standing.
I'm in transition,
A reset,
A redo.
A small lapse rewind.
I'm owning of an era of wrongs,
I'm in search to claim the right.
I've secured an epic amount of courage.
Just enough to make my soul take flight.
You see-
I'm in transition.
Changes are afoot.

Hustle Poet

The kind that make you better,
Once you rid your soul of the soot.
There's no longer a need to burn your memory,
You've torched the heart house you made in flames,
I've taken full responsibility now,
I'm owning the full blame.
Yes, it's me who is in transition.
It's me who needed the change.
A blooming flower cannot grow in toxic surroundings,
When it's your poison seeping in my veins.
It's me who needed to leave the mess of you,
You won't pull me down any further now.
I won't have to watch you drown your shame.

I'm in transition.
I've truly been through so much.
For 3 years I put up with your vicissitude,
I've stomached the worst of your bad luck.
I'm making alterations now,
Modifying the parts you made dead inside.
I no longer have to dim my light anymore,
My identity I no longer have to hide.

I'm in transition,
Interchanging is no longer needed.
There's no time limit added now,
No pressure to make sure you succeed.

I'm done hiding your shortcomings,
Your flattered flaws,
Your epic misgivings.

In transition

I'm no longer at fault now,
When they find you OD'ing on a floor.
You'll just be the guy who taught me,
The one who gave up on life,
The one who always maintained a score.
I'm not ungrateful for the lessons learned along the
journey,
You've taught me so many things,
Most important thing I learned in my transition,
You taught me to wish for someone more.

I'm in transition now,
Embracing the altering need for change,
When others ask for you in passing,
I simply won't remember your name.

Legacy

Say their name.
Realize it's not you who can assign blame,
Notice we all have a choice.
A person's demise doesn't give anyone a reason to commit
crimes or rejoice.
It's more than an past-tense addendum to a Destiny's child
song,
It's not a call-to-action for those who have been wronged.
Don't allow anyone to make your premeditated choices.
There is a correct way to utilize the power of your words,
A better use for the strength of your voice.

Say their name,
Raise it in glory,
In peace,
In honor.

Say it with some respect.
Say it so the world will never be able to forget.
It's more than just a tragedy.
This is a severe lesson.
This is not how God's children behave.
Have some respect for yourself before you curse the
strength of your own name.

Say their name,
Loud and clear-
Say it so their life becomes more than a legacy,
Not just a mark deemed erasable,
Not an acceptable close,
Not a goal,

Hustle Poet

Not a reason to embrace or instate a society wide new normal.

Say their name.
They are important-
Just like every life in existence.
They were people,
Loved,
Needed and treasured.
They are more than examples of how a person's purpose can become deceitful.

Say their name.
Give it power.
Watch how intention can give someone more than just a steeple.

Say their name,
Pause in reflection.
Say a prayer for those whose anger has overtaken them,
The ones who grieve,
Terrified of what is to come for those with the same appearance others can't understand,

The ones whose rage begets ignorance....
Turning Presidential tweet filled lies into fearful facts of fake news in droves.
Don't allow his weak ignorance to write looting checks your ass can't cash.

Say their name.

Legacy

Be grateful for your existence,
Despite the state the world decides to drift in.
Become inspired to enact change instead of becoming a
burden too heavy to write history in.

Say their name,
When the "everyone is doing it" excuses slip in.
Be on the right side of history,
Be on the peaceful side of the divide.

Remember which shoes you fit in,
Remember to make sure you're not the reason others have
to run and hide.
Realize-
You're not protesting if you're looting,
stealing or committing crimes.
You're breaking the law.
Robbing other people,
Taking other's lives.
Killing people-
That means you're just as guilty as the opposition,
You're just like the enemy you view in the grass is greener
filled eyes. Making that choice-
You've lost the reason to riot,
Lost the dignity that is carried by race.

SAY THEIR NAME-
the next time you make a choice to be hateful.
It's their memory,
Their meaning,
Their legacy for change you now disgrace.

Hustle Poet

Say their name.
Remember who you are.
It's what you choose to stand for that will tell the measure
of a person you are.
If you can't remember,
Ask yourself this:
If you were in their place . . .
Muttering the plea . . .
"I CAN'T BREATHE",
Calling for your mama,
Trying to beg for help as others witness the moments a
child of God leaves . . .
Will there be someone rioting in your name?
Will someone protest peaceful for you?
Would they march, demanding justice for your life or
would your actions define your death-
Silencing the right for anyone to speak?

Say their name,
Do the right thing,
Make sure the choices you make don't leave your known
legacy to be criminal, disgraceful and weak.

Climax Your Cause.

Climax Your Cause

Purpose Picket,
That's how we sell tickets.
We raise our voice informing our goals,
We will inspire you to care,
You'll pick up a picket sign,
Encourage you to share.

We will shout to the heavens,
We will force them to hear us,
We won't move until change comes,
We will make them fear us.

We fight for civil rights,
We dare you to try & discourage our order.
Our voice makes a difference now,
We will outnumber their borders.

Strike,
Strike,
Don't Cross our line.
With each vote they make law now,
Our climate continues to decline.
Scabs,
Scabs,
You're not enforcing our plan.
How can you cross our line now?
On these issues you choose where you stand.
Don't be discouraged,
When you see our line,
Ask for information on the causes.

Hustle Poet

Ask about the projects.
Ask why.
Ask about the laws that effect more than just youth & children,
How would you feel if that was your future to live in?

Slogan,
Slogan,
We all should join in.
We fight for our future,
Our state of the union,
We fight for energy control,
We fight for all walks of life.

You have a voice,
Don't be ashamed to use it.
Become a participating part of a strike we call life.

We strike for civil rights,
To help support the frontline youth leaders,
We fight for our climate,
#100 is now,
Don't let them deceive you.
We fight for treaties.
Biodiversity,
Environmental injustices,
We fight for equal pay.

We fight for the right for you to have a future,
What good is a planet without the human race?
Raise up your voice,
Don't just climax your climate,
Before it's too late.

Climax Your Cause

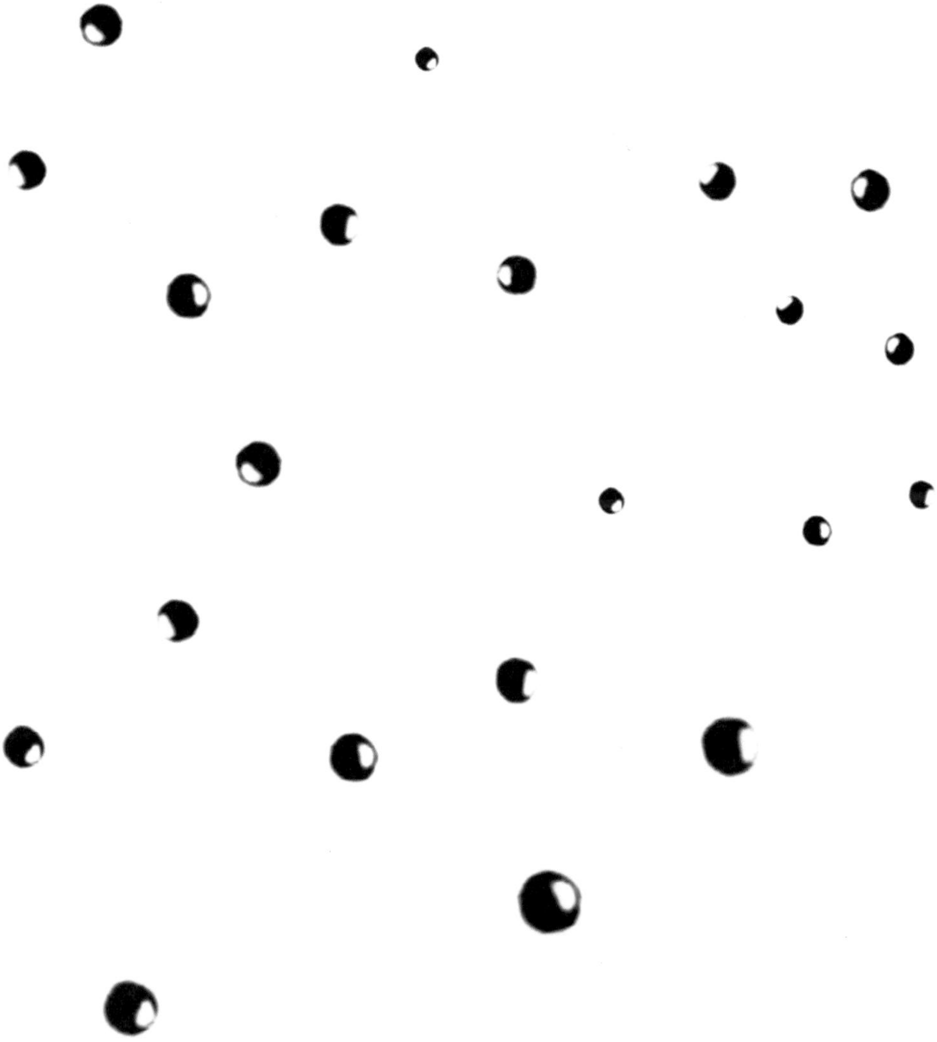

If life and death are in the power of my tongue,
May my tongue immortalize you in favor.
If life and death stems from the root of my words,
May the fruit or my words that nourishes your soul be sweetened to
satisfy the monster inside you.

If life and death are deeply seeded in the fruits of my linguistic favor
run as deep as wellspring waters,
May the harvest that springs from my lips fill your cup,
 Lavish your soul,
Captivate your mind while feeding the hunger that passion drives.

If life and death are interwoven in the fabric of your silver lining,
May you be dressed in elegance to slay a thousand souls.

If life and death spring from life s I create fruit of the lips,
 Quenching the spoils of the ambrosia vine,
May your life be ten thousand times the many divine.
For it is the words you read that line my soul,
Capture my purpose,
Identify my grace while spreading the kiss that lines a million
foreheads.

May you ever be blessed & bathed in lyrical truth,
Clothe your back with righteousness,
And line your path with destined wisdom
to always find your way home.

If life and death are in the power of your truth,
May you always remember who you are,
No matter what rises in the road to greet you.

Society

Society is not my favorite place.
In all my years of living,
I've learned lessons along the way.
Some truth-filled,
Some deceiving,
This place is like wearing the cone of shame.
The sight of what's left of society is a complete disgrace.

We walk around daily,
Among people of our chosen environment,
So eager to measure ourselves,
Against a scale that has been tipped in the favor of the
violent.

I sit and watch the actions of many,
I ponder what drove them to react so petty.
My guess is they aren't able to be held accountable.

They anger so quickly when I call them to the table,
Upset because I refuse to lower my standard to allow them
to be able, Because I refuse accept false excuses as
payment for truth.

Society is not my favorite place.
It just so happens that statement is the full ugly truth,
Didn't everyone learn about taking accountability way
back in their youth? Is that not something our elders try to
teach?
It's secreted in there among the thou shall's…
They try to show us the way without trying to preach.
If you sit quietly, thinking about their actions vs yours,

Hustle Poet

You'll begin to see how much falseness you actually
endure.

Hindsight is a MF.
It teaches you valuable lessons.
If you're not careful,
Your pity for them will get you asking yourself questions.

You'll start to analyze their words filled with false reasons,
You'll start to pinpoint the moment they committed
treason.
You start to wonder if the wolves dig the sheep's threads
they sleep in.

Then, you'll laugh to yourself,
Realizing why you could never invest in them.
You start to question the azimuth of your own compass.
If they mistake your kindness for meanness,
Shouldn't that make their worth to you redundant?

Society is not my favorite place.
It's filled with imposters.
Ever notice the moment they point the finger,
It's usually because they're mad they are not allowed to
linger?

They leave willingly,
Make no mistake about that.
They fire themselves among inspired flames,
quickly turn into a victim from crimes they commit,
Ready to trick whoever has time to hear them blame.

Society

Yeah, I'm the mean girl,
The one who asks for the well-being of others,
The one who gives chances,
Despite the opinions of Mothers.

I have many given titles,
By people who stand for nothing.

A narcissist,
A mean girl,
A woman who is wicked,
I don't sink to their level.
I don't swim in the shame lake they drown in.

I just smile and nod,
Paddle my boat in the other direction.
You can't receive your blessings sitting in another's stress
mess.

Thank them kindly for their unsolicited opinions,
Give em a "God bless you",
Wish them the best of luck.

Some people will sink themselves,
All you have to do is watch & not give a fuck.
Don't worry about giving them a life raft,
Don't worry about the sins they seed.
You will see clearly which wolf they chose to feed.
Don't worry about what will rise to meet them in their
chosen road of destruction,
That's how society is now,

Hustle Poet

That's how lesser people adapt to function,
To exist,
To survive,
Remember- When the shit gets thick,
When you lose people you considered friends,
So close they could be family,
Stay kind even when they mistreat or misconstrue your actions.

Don't let society change your nature,
Praise those you consider important to feature.
Wear the titles they give you with pride,
Don't return their hatefulness.

Hold your head high,
Take it in stride.
Smile, wave & wink when they show you their monster inside.

Don't allow yourself to be hateful or bitter,
Be resplendent.
There's a reason they can't stand the light you are blessed in.
When they fall,
it's no longer your responsibility.
when they fail to thrive-
Just wear those society titles they gave you,
To their negative presence turn a blind eye.

Hustle Poet

The Cutting Board

In a world filled with opportune mess,
I cover my body with evidence of distress.
Scars of love,
Slices of care,
They aren't meant to garner your stares.

Words evade me,
My mind becomes silent.
Small Incisions release the hope I keep hidden.
The numbness spreads like a warm mink blanket,
Each cut covers my numbered worries,
A welcomed distraction.

The rush of endorphins kidnaps my feelings,
A wound in the exterior of who I must pretend to be.
A secreted cause in a chain of outs,
These cuts perfectly placed are my version of pouts.

The pureness of bleeding,
Added to a long list of therapy I've been self-treating.
Slicing away the taste of hate,
The flavor of vile,
The arrogance of disgrace.

I'm still alive,
I can feel,
Through these scars my purity can heal.

The stillness of impact,
My lonesome habit,
It has zero to do with life losing measures,

Hustle Poet

It's now a force of habit.

The second rush of endorphins,
My curiosity remains piqued,
I only cut in the shadows,
The places no one can see.

My pain is not dormant,
It's palpable,
It's real,
It reminds me I am alive,
My cuts serve as a reminder of times I needed to feel the
rush of my thrive.

Sometimes it's not for coping,
It's more than just a mechanism.
Sometimes it's an acceptable diversion to make sure the
truth doesn't get in.
It hurts to be loved,
Especially when you don't feel needed.

It's not some morbid romance,
No suicidal cuts are needed.
It's an addiction to a knife,
The sharpened edges of a ten blade or a razor,
I'm simply cutting out the parts of me,
The parts I don't like.

These scars are my truth,
I don't see a body defiled.
I see a release of freedom,

The Cutting Board

The opening of flesh,
My hidden ceremonial pastime.

When you see as a person in distress,
Don't think of my scars as a crime.
Think of them as moments,
Times bravery felt defeated.

These scars tell my story,
A history worth hearing,
Allow me a moment to tell you the truth you're evading.

I'm a cutting board.
I've been cut down to the core,
Be careful with my spirit as it is me you try to restore.
Don't fill me with your perceptions,
These scars aren't a reflection of a lack of religion,
I've been a child of God my whole life,
It's not me who is trying to fit you in.

Sometimes it's deeper than the family you exist in.
Be patient as you learn why each cut was put in scores,
I am loved by God,
The proof is in each healed cut His love has restored.

Word Murdered

Word Murdered

I Word murdered you,
just to get you to breathe.
I Word murdered you,
Just to allow your soul to let me sleep.

I word murdered you,
Simply because I couldn't allow you to kill me.
My words filled with anger pierced your soul.
I found out the only way to get your attention Was to shock
you,
In a vast effort to leave you shook.
You'd see more than just the pretty face you adore,
You'd see me.
You'd see the woman who is no longer afraid to Shake
your tree.

The woman who savored the craving of your fruit.
The woman who drove her sword into what is left of you.
The woman who revealed your soured core.
Yes,
Beloved.
I word murdered you.
That version of you needed to die.
That monster inside that lingered,
Hovering,
Quaking,
That constant Hyde to the kindness of your mysterious
Jekyll.
I word murdered both of your faces.
It wasn't me who is gonna leave this world
among a mountain of the disgraced.

Hustle Poet

I couldn't go toward without showing you
the kindness of murdering purity.
You killed my pure heart,
Burned the human part of me in effigy.

For a small fragment of time,
The monster inside you laughed,
You danced a tribal Braille tribute.
The only way to get through to you is to give you
 words your soul cannot dispute.

I know I hurt you,
With the velocity of my words.
I won't say I'm sorry,
I acknowledge the hurt.
 I word murdered you as a sacrifice,
Saving anyone else from the threat of your lips that entice.

I word murdered you justly,
For three years I walked your line,
Knowing I should have ran from you.
My heels were stuck the moment your heart reached out for
mine.
Your heart caressed my soul
like it was bathing me in the lapses of your mind.
The silent moments secreted between your heart beats,
That's the day my love was sold.
Remember how we planned together to grow old?
To raise a bunch of babies,
Little monsters with eyes of blue,
With your russet hair shining,

Word Murdered

With my dimples,
The world would be threw.

You weren't someone I anticipated outgrowing,
I word murdered you without anyone knowing.
I stayed-
In truth-
 Longer than I should have.

 I should have poisoned you softly,
Slowly step away from my innocent crime.
I stayed to comfort the child in you.
Because in you- I see the divine.
It's not that I don't love you.
I do-
So deeply,
So unconditional-
You are all I'd ever need.
I love you more than most,
More than anyone could ever dream.
I love you so entirely-
The one person I lost was me.
I word murdered you, darling,
To get you to understand that you matter,
To get you to notice the pain you put inside me,
To get someone other than you to react.
I word murdered you simply to keep my heart intact.

I used to love him,
I adored him like a precious gem.
I lived for him like I was born into a world of whimsical
miracles.
I'd count our blessings until they were multiplied by ten.

I used to love him,
Infatuated,
Intoxicated by his words.
I counted myself lucky,
Measured myself against the race of a dollar,
Grateful to be 15 cents.

I counted myself blessed to be his addiction,
Not realizing the cost of that high.
I counted myself used to loving him,
Until the day my skies fell.

I counted my tune deceased,
Deadened,
Finished,
Left famished for the hunger of his tainted apologies I
counted the apologies that I've become accustomed to.
One by one,
Filling by emptied cup.
I counted the seconds it took my music box to realize it was
left asunder.
That was a sorrowful day.
My wind-chime slowed,
My ballerina bellowed.
Her graceful spinning ceased.

Hustle Poet

No dance followed,
I wanted to die right there,
No one was left to coddle.

She simply embraced the new world we needed,
The world we didn't want to endure.
I wasn't sure I could count anymore,
I had to be sure.

What I found when I went searching was more than
alluring,
I lost myself loving him,
That was the painful truth I've been murmuring.

I lost my sense of direction,
I lost my true north,
I lost my mind according to my conscious,
It was my ballerina I had to help catch her wind.

I lost him to love myself.
That's how I learned to win.
So when your heart reminds your soul,
When you have problems remembering your goal,
Remember how you used to love yourself,
Before encountering his monstrous soul.

Tortured

Tortured

I've watched him with careful eyes,
Studying each structured curve his hands offered.
It was like an addiction I couldn't seduce my thoughts
away from. Strong yet gentle.
Tracing the movements of your touch.
Captivated, I was intoxicated by your brilliant words.
A spoken word poet.
His words seeped into me heavy with Intent.

My attention claimed, Instantly, I'm shook.
Yes, I noticed.
He is Remarkable.
He moved my spirit the same way the wind caresses
melody into trees. My branches not needing to be swayed.

I was willing,
Fighting against the current of want,
Held hostage by conceptual musings of doubt when his
voice sang my name like a holy hymn. Who is he truly?
I was burning with filthy wonder,
Do my deceitful eyes lie in the midst of want?
I needed to possess the light that enchanted every inch of
you.
My heart pounding,
My mind considering-
Perplexed by this Adonis tribute with cobalt blue eyes.

Battling to embrace my secreted thoughts,
My eyes traced every second of his building smile.
Aqua Di Gio.

Hustle Poet

The scent sent to slay the dragon that guards my heart.
Struggling to keep my legs from trembling beneath me,
Aching to get away,
I stayed to brave the outcome.

I longed to be burned by the fire his lips charmed.
There was no denying his sorcery,
He claimed my soul the second his eyes met mine.
Panicking- I struggled to remember my words.
No, lover.. I'm not seeing anyone.
My small nervous laugh enticed him,
Piquing his curiosity once more.
I've been yours since your tongue tasted my name,
I breathed,
Breathlessly & managed,
Confident In stride,
I gathered my pride,
walked away victorious,
Celebrating in silence with unanticipated fervor.
His voice calling out to me,
Stopping me in my tracks.

His words-
This is how our story begins,
Shall I stow my sword
Or should I let my love attack?
My smile betrayed me once more,
A rosy hue covering my dimpled cheeks,
My mahogany eyes shined,
Shimmering back to reveal my crush.
He knew I loved the feeling of being tortured,

Tortured

My heart I gave to him in trust.

I've been tortured,
Captivated in love,
From the first moment I heard new love speak.

Hustle Poet

Scars

My scars mean more than just me
  being stronger than whatever tried to hurt me.
My scars are the marks of know-how,
They are the marks of an epic success of a failure.
They are the marks that represent the times
  I notice people don't listen,
They are thinking of things to say when it's their turn to
talk,
Their turn prove,
Their turn to attempt to move me with their narcissistic
vision.
They are the marks of proof I lived,
Marks that prove I matter.

Pay attention to the patterns of tormented skin.
Pay attention to the scars I've hidden deep within.
My scars tell the story of people,
My chosen people.
People who live to hate me when I'm too real,
When I'm too legit to lie, cheat and steal.

It's those same people who embrace the fake,
Trying to see others within me like my honesty is a
mistake.

My scars tell a story of power,
They show the days I was brave,
They show the struggle I refuse to empower.
My scars show the choice of the day I chose to live Over
the overwhelming Willingness to die.

Hustle Poet

My scars broke my heart,
But fixed my vision.
My scars saved me.
I look at them now to remind me of my decision.

I chose to survive,
I chose to deal,
No matter what comes,
just like my scars-
I will always heal.

Change

Affirm. Repeat. Change.

I am love.
I have no color.
I am abundance.
I have no preference.
I am choice.
I have no boundaries.
I am future.
I am endless.
I am the Pureness or sight.
I have no prejudice.
I am inspiration.
I have no discrimination clauses.
I am motivation.
I have no limits.
I am race.
I have no bias.
I am infinite.
I have every option.
I am victorious.
I have known a fighter's mentality.
I am family.
I have bled knowing you.
I am solid.
I have acquired strength by injustice.
I am a failure.
I have reached success many times.
I am broken.
I have known the weight of cost.
I am determined.

Hustle Poet

I have known struggle.
I am the dream.
Because I have seen myself in your eyes.
I am change.

I have challenged my perception to become what the world
needs.

It starts with you.

Words become thoughts.
Thoughts become actions.
Actions bring about change.
Do something your legacy will be known for.
Earn the right to say your name.

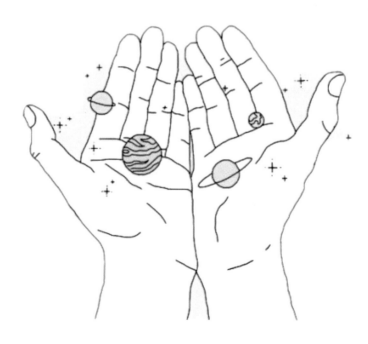

Motto

I was born for greatness.
Made fearless,
Formed by struggle,
Molded by faith.

I was born to walk the path of the righteous,
Already dying,
Humbled from a young age.

Determined to outshine those who deny my ability,
Designed to teach those who question their own steps.
Turned away by those who are damaged by their own
choices, Questioned by those who struggle with their own
faith.
Feared by those who don't know what their purpose Is.

I was born remarkable, Shaped in the image of my
ancestors.
I accept the path laid out before me,
Willingly, I step by blind faith into my future,
Longing,
Knowing,
Understanding That I was born strong,
Filled with the strength God gave me to survive this world.
I swim because It doesn't suit me to sink.
I go forward,
Nodding to the past that contributed to the person I am
now.
I was born grateful,
Destined to grow in love among hate,
Speaking life into those who'd rather witness me dead.

Hustle Poet

The opinion of many may state a lot of riddled phrases,
The one statement I will always claim:
I was born to be an original.

Affirm it.
Know it.
Love it.
Live it.

A CUP OF GET SHIT DONE

The Secret

The Secret

She doesn't know,
The secret you savor,
The quiet climax you Favor..
She can't see,
Her vision blinded by faith in her husband,
A violator of innocent trust,
Blinded by the betrayal of your looks.

She can't see the mistress seated in the row marked three.
Your lust filled tells.
I've got a collection of tryst stories that'll sell.

The secret you savor,
Seasoned with devious flavor.
It burns,
Always having to wait my turn.
The lies,
The deceit,
The toll of deceiving,
My photos are constantly screened.

The hoops I jump are riddled with receipts.
No I get it, baby,
You're held by obligations.
By her death threats,
Her feigned suicide by dull knives.

Your love to her is rationed,
It's my love for you that'll be her surprise.
It feels good to be bad,
It feels worse to be sided.

Hustle Poet

A side piece of no peace,
An additional secreted partner,
A failure of accountability to barter.

I am reduced to being a minus,
A subtraction of moments lost.
A less then of mistress cent bonus,
A lipstick list Vision.

The secret you savor,
It's too late.
We love each other.
We can't repent,
Our secret drowns each other.
Its evidence we can't leave,
There's no telling what lies from your lips she will believe.
No conscious to be checked,
lips of an angel with dirty demon tendencies.
Here's to my secret,
A secret ode to the woman I'll never be.
The woman in the next room,
The second woman in a forced,
secret polyamorous affair of three.

Secreted calls,
Hiding behind a barrier to walls.
Hushed words wishing she were me.
Her calls are audible,
Mine vibrate in threes.

The secret you savor,

The Secret

The things I've done to gain your favor.
You dream of me,
Betrayal of sleepily saying my name.
What makes you think she doesn't know?

The secret you savor.
I am the weakness of your blame,
The one who places scratches down your back,
The reason she is forced to hack,
You claim to love I have to give,
 I leave you hungry,
starving for attention.
I make you miss me.

Unfortunately for you –
The secret I savor,
I'm not the kind to keep you.
I'm the kind you cannot see when I want.
The kind who lives her fantasy in hours,
Simply because you are a man who cowers.
I give you back every night,
Praying your absence starts a fight.

The secret I savor,
I've done naughty things to keep your favor.
I'm the woman who is gifted Flowers,
The woman who provides the sweetness to your sours.

I don't want you permanently,
You're just for fun.
Don't need to be sealed with rings of fire.

Hustle Poet

I am the woman who answers your every burning desire.

Now I'm seated in the same room with the woman who
shares your name,
She smiles at me not knowing,
The secret I savor,
I'm the reason for her pain.

We've shared the same days,
Repeated different nights,
The difference today being when I tell her,
It's too late- You can't save her.
Now she'll know I'm the woman,
The secret you savor.

Hustle Poet

Wanted

131

Wanted

I want . . . Honesty.
The same kind of truth I spoon feed you daily.
The kind of truth that's more plausible than a maybe.

I want. . . The look of innocence,
The resilient look of honest hope that lingers in your
determined eyes.

I want. . . Function.
You're more than just an average routine of an eventual
fact.
The same kind of actions true love takes to show a woman
the lining of your antiquated soul.

I want. . . Beneficial.
The same kind of gain you receive from taking every ounce
of energy and light I have to give.

I want. . . More than just commitment.
The same adoration that faces you when my smile lingers a
little bit too long on eager lips.

I want. . . Your words.
The same kind of exclamations of inspiration I draw from
basking in the glow of your hunted spirit.
I create from your darkness.

I want. . . Your desires.
The kind of sentiments that move more than just my spirit.
The kind that light your fire.
I need your words that make me think,

Hustle Poet

I need your emotions like you need to sync.

I want. . . Respect.
The same kind of respect you used to fight your anger.
The kind where rational thought me to extreme passion.
That's the kind of love worth dying for,
The kind I'd kindly give my life to even the score.
The kind I swim this season over for ten times more.

I want. . . More than just empty love.
The kind of amorous existence that causes your heart to
question your soul.
The kind of love that empowers,
Not enslaves,
Not love I'd have to harvest like it's your heart I stole.

I want. . . Remembrance.
The kind act of recalling this very moment –
That way the next time the situational conversation arises,
You can say with certainty,
With conviction,
With absolutely no surprises,
A strong woman just blessed you,
enlightened you,
Empowered you,
Take the lesson we know best in.
You now know what our stance is,
There's no need next time to act like you're frontin'.
A woman just gave you a blueprint of what women have
always wanted.

Hustle Poet

Soda

My cat is an asshole,
Yeah, I said it.
Our skin is torn to shreds,
No one is safe walking,
we are used as a scratch pole.

My cat is an asshole,
A betrayer of the house of Vaughan.
The mischievous little cat bag,
This is the tale of pussycat name Soda Vaughan.

Soda Aloysius Vaughan,
First of his name,
Born of the foofi fluff,
A warrior of catnip forest.
We received soda as a gift before we knew what was before
us.

My cat is an asshole,
Dark as night,
A known knife fighter,
decorated with a stripe of white.
He's nice for a moment,
White paws fast as lightning,
What I know now is twice as frightening.

Soda Vaughan,
He's an angry little elf,
I'm convinced he's Lucifer in cat form.
Also known as the conqueror of shelves and shape shifting,

Hustle poet

I go to bed worrying,
He's waiting to catch me slipping.

My cat is an asshole,
The fluffy slayer of ankles and toes,
Thank goodness we love him more than he knows.

Soda Vaughan,
An angry little thief,
There's so much in the story,
There's many reasons we have beef.
The bearer of orange eyes glaring at me from with in the dark,
If he had thumbs,
He'd set fire to my clothes with just one spark.

My cat is an asshole,
The terror of Vaughan Manor.
I bottle-fed this lunatic with an attitude tooo rude to handle.

If Soda could talk,
He'd speak of pure scandal.
I'm living on borrowed days,
The truth- I swear I thought I saw him panhandle.
Are you in the market for a noisy, nosy feline familiar?
I'll give him to you willingly.
I'll pack his shit,
his food,
his fancy bottled water and his toys.

I'm sure one day with soda will fill your life with joy.

His nails are sharp as a razor,
last Thursday I found out he likes to be tasered,
He scratched up my ankle tattoo so bad it has to be lasered.

My cat is a glorious asshole,
I think you might have more luck,
On second thought,
If he leaves- Our family would be lost,
I guess I'll stomach the asshole.
The asshole we aren't allowed to touch,
I suppose we will keep him,
we've grown to love him SO much.
The asshole.

Mirror

What's in a friend?
A favor.
A journey.
I'm learning my path to awesomeness is quite situational
and lonely.
I tried to catch the reason,
Reasons you hang around me solely.

What's in a friend?
Do I intrigue your mind?
Do I place you in trances?
I take note of each of you,
I've numbered your side glances.
Does it make you feel good doubting all my techniques and
skills,
Just for the sake of achieving secret thrills?

Does disliking what's different garner your audience?
What will happen to you once your friends see through
your disguises? I'd hate to see what happens when they see
through your defenses.

What's a friend?
Is it honor?
Is it your idea of poor planning?
Your bullying doesn't stop the person I'm growing to be.
No matter what you do –
I'm always going to be me.

What's in a friend?
You obviously don't know Dash Don't worry –

Hustle Poet

I'll tell you.
A friend is the person who sees you,
The person you make fun of incessantly.
A friend is someone who likes you,
Stands up for you,
Even when the words you choose are ugly.

Words are powerful,
Don't bully someone different or new.
Be careful which words you choose.
A friend is someone who is talking to you,
Someone who's trying to get through.

Hustle Poet

Capcity

Capacity

I need the capacity. . .
The space to forget you.
To walk-
Free.
I need the moment,
To exhale through my tears,
Memories that haunt me,
the courage to relive our years.

I need the capacity. . .
The movement to fill this void.
I'm done searching the endless musings,
I refuse the lasting Anagrams I want to piece together to
cope.

I need the capacity. . .
The chance to let go.
I'm sick of your influence from before.
I don't wanna love you anymore.

I'm done giving you hope.

I need the capacity. . .
The room to make needed changes.
I fight off thoughts of you daily,
Normal days now feel strange.

I need the capacity. . .
A day in the sun,
I'm yearning for a calm place to breathe,
I'm done being taught how to run.

Hustle Poet

I need the capacity. . .
An opportunity to run out of blue.
It's getting easier to forget the taste of your lips now,
The taste of sweet salt in your tears,
I'll keep saying it until it's true.

I now have the capacity. . .
I've embraced the person you made me become.
I see you in your truest form.
I've seen the truth behind all of your scars.
I'm past the pushover lovesick bad man you claim you
have reformed. I'm not your claim to fame.
I'm not your charity case.
I'm The right one to expose the pictures you try to paint.
 I'll lay all your indiscretions In the light,
This battle is over now,
For you- I no longer fight.

When you see me passing,
Don't Gawk.
Don't stutter,
Don't try it, Motherfucka.

I now have the capacity,
The motives,
The clarity,
The skill to end you.
I replaced every ounce of you with someone real.
Someone who will never be you.

Someone who I will always appreciate,

Capacity

Someone for who I will always try.

Now...
Find the ability to stay far away,
Find the capacity to figure out why.

Future

Future

I am the future,
The constant range of change.
I am the stance of righteous,
Your actions now will become the blame.

I am the youth,
Watching with widening eyes.
I am the consequence you shape with all of your lies.

I am the path,
The caution at your feet.
The world is more important than rioting in the streets.
You fight for our future,
Fighting for an outcome of change.
Your litter lines the street to storm,
Replacing your cause with shame.

I am the future,
What is the truth you are teaching me?
Does your social conscious plate make your tofu saltier
with time?
Don't you realize –
It's me you influence by design.
Quick to follow Greta as she speaks forest filled words
with conviction.
How do your False words taste as you try to define your
mission?
At what point do you do self-checks and question your
fired passions?
I'm the one girl you cannot lie to.
Saving the world is more than just in fashion.

Hustle Poet

It's not a fad.
Not a hipster,
not cute,
not a lasting joke.
I'm bothered.

The more the trees burn our air,
The more our future is destined to choke.

I am the future,
I'm pissed off,
I am sickened and saddened.

We need to be better as people,
Our planet needs our passion.
In the words of Greta Thunberg –
We'll be watching you,
How dare you.

My future dreams are worth saving.
My childhood is filled with suffering.

hey lady –
Put down your phone.
This message isn't made for the person watching,
For them to sit through the buffering.
This is a message from the future,
The dream left to March and carry the torch on this planet.
A change that is worth what's coming.
We will not allow you to fail us,
My life is not a future I'm selling.

Brevity

151

Brevity

Concealed in the continuation of your brevity,
I saw your faith,
And an ounce of clarity,
I understood the emptiness.
The tragedy you hold onto.
The weakness that holds you back.

Concealed in the continuation of your brevity,
I found strength.
I stumbled upon reason.
I tripped over your conscious that was pacing to hide its
season.

For a lapse in the extra seconds I stole,
I witnessed a mirror image of you,
I saw your ghost.
It hovered in place,
A remembrance of someone I once new.
I quaked inside whispering in wonder-
How could this be true?

I've witnessed the death of someone I thought I knew.
Concealed in the continuation of your brevity,
I stood confused,
I rambled,
staring down a bewildered soul.
If only I could reach you,
If only you allowed me to help you grow.

My heart had hoped to heal you,
My love I tried to sew,

Hustle Poet

To repair the cuts within you,
That way your scars wouldn't show.

Concealed in the continuation of my brevity,
You will find a pathway filled with broken hearts,
Shattered musings,
Broken records,
An account of every time you misused me.

Concealed in the continuation of my brevity,
You'll discover more than just a person who loved you,
You'll stumble upon a person who never even the score.

You'll find enlightenment,
A light in the darkness for the lost souls I tried to help,
you'll find a shadow of a murdered version of me to
weakened to matter.
Concealed in the continuation of my brevity,

You'll unveil the truth.
You'll find the meaning of life I once provided,
The one that almost ended me as I found my truth.

Concealed in the continuation of our brevity,
We found freedom,
We found the willingness to finally let go.
We found courage to do the kind thing,
We found the strength to admit it was time to accept what
we both knew.

In the continuation of brevity,

I found someone I once knew.
I found the woman destroyed by loving you.
I found my voice to say no.

Ode To A Pill.

Ode to a Pill

I crave your numbness,
The warmth you made me feel,
I crave your abilities,
The abilities that stops me from being able to feel.

I crave the fuzziness that surrounds me in darkness.
I crave the silence,
To silence all the voices.

I need the newness.
The discovery of things unseen.
I need the protection you give,
You shield me from those that are mean.

I miss the ritual.
The feeling of having you in my pocket.
The chalkiness of your stain,
The bitter murkiness of your taste.

I miss being unaware to what happens in real time.
I miss the feeling of your body melting on my tongue,
I miss the thoughts of one more pill and I'm done.
I missed the secret,
The hidden fact of being an addict.

I even miss the accusations of being a junkie,
A name no one really fathoms,
It just kind of happens.
They don't stop and think –
They are the reason you seek the numbness.

Hustle Poet

They are the reason you're always know where one hits.
It's not a disease.
It's a choice one makes.
it's the person who puts that pill on their tongue,
It's the person who chooses to make life become undone.

There's a choice to make before you pull that trigger.
There's more to life,
More things to consider.

Be careful when making these life path decisions,
There's some choices you can't take back,
Some that robs you of your vision.

Know the truth- Fully without bias.
Be kind with yourself.
Don't be irrational.
There's always a way to correct your mistakes.
It's you who holds the keys,
it's you who chooses which path to take.

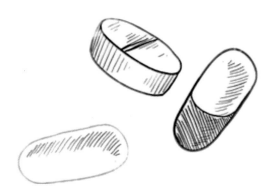

Tin Foil Princess

Tin Foil Princess

I need someone who looks at me like magic,
Who's dealt with everything tragic.
I need more than Prince Charming,
I need a twisted version of Prince Valiant.
I need the majestic vision in tinfoil so gleaming,
I'll need to look twice and damn near piss myself,
Convinced I'm still dreaming.

I need the dude who's smile Chings in rhythmic wonder.
the dude who would never steal my thunder.
I need the dude who is flawless yet imperfect,
So dashing.
I need someone who looks at me with pizzazz.
Who glares at me with wonder.

I need the guy who will get tased with me and not spazz.
the guy who would laugh with me in complete stitches,
At everything and nothing just the same.
I need the guy who won't be pissed when I can't remember
his name.
the majestical unicorn beast with chin length hair,
the guy who busts out steps like Fred Astaire.

I need the guy who isn't afraid to say he's sorry.
I'll agree he's sorry too…
Just in case I need a cover story.
I need the guy who is patient and kind,
The guy who hears every last word I say,
Noting a few "yes, dear" when I vent while spilling my
wine.

Hustle Poet

I need the guy who is compassionate like Keanu.
Who will kill a MF dead if he upset me by disrespecting his
woman-
even if it's true.

I need a guy who will knock me off my socks...
Someone brave enough to thrill me.

I need the guy who isn't afraid to tell me I'm a pain in the ass,
a guy who lives for all 231 phases of my sass.
I need the guy who will scare me just to see me scream,
the guy who isn't rude or mean.

I need the guy who will always pretend to be stroked.
The one who will rectify any situation being broke.
It sounds like a tall order-
My majestical magnificent magical gazing at me guy…
I want whomever God sends to me.

I'll try my best not to laugh when I make him cry.
I'll be doting-
for a moment,
Let's not get hasty.
I'll make him happy,
Slip a happy pill in his chili-
maybe?
I'd sit through all the reasons I can't own a sugar glider named
Divine.
Don't underestimate the power of my love,
I can make him just as crazy as I am . . .
with time.

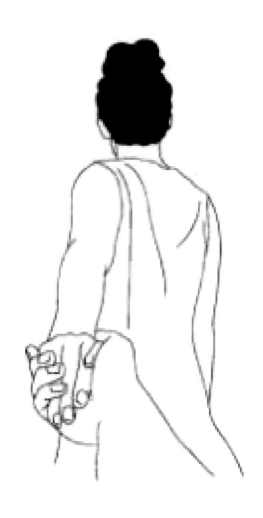

Mantra

Mantra

Nothing wasted,
Nothing acquired.
I chased down an idea of something inspired,
Misdiagnosing love is something required.

Nothing wasted,
Nothing learned.

It's a constant worry of what goes unearned.
Does he love me?

Do I even care?
The concern of yearning internally –
A disaster of numerous money.

How does one maintain a life worth living when so many choose
to remain petty?

Nothing wasted,
Nothing deserved.

It's all a big game now,
Victorious is far from goals.
Perception of the masses is lost.
Is placing your image –
Your life on the 'gram-
Worth all the identity that is lost?
Nothing wasted,
Nothing gained.

The lack of empathy and others is often the culprit of blame.

Hustle Poet

Why continue to starve for something if your motivation
daily is declining?

Can you hear what I'm telling you?
Read closer between the lines.
If there's nothing wasted in the attention you used to
Comprehend,
You just gained new perspective,
You just gained a new friend.

You now have the motivation to try.
If nothing is wasted and following your ambition,
next line realize how strong you are despite your reason,
conviction or disposition.
You have the ability to acquire knowledge,
You have the lessons to help you maintain.

You will achieve the greatness you deserve,
Everyone will come to know your name.
You have nothing to waste,
You have everything to attain.

The ball is in your court now.
Choose your actions wisely.
The outcome depends on the path you choose to maintain.
It depends on living a life worth the pain.

Amaarah Gray

American Writer/Poet/Screenwriter/Producer.

Accomplished World Traveler, Speaker, Author, Veteran, 3rd Degree Blackbelt World Champion, Writer, Poet, Producer& Avid Shoe Wearer, who is a die-hard RedSox fan. In that order.

Member of the International Association of Professional Women.

Born in 1980, Amaarah launched her career as a Writer in November of 2012 with several titles under another Nom De Plume, exploring different avenues of storytelling & 25 scripts to date. Taking a creative approach, Amaarah writes to inspire the world with a suggestion of a new perception amidst adversity that has been crafted, cultivated, and released in poetic verse to caress real thoughts, actions, perspective, and wisdom into the minds of every reader who is in search of truth, guidance, and a new voice to gain understanding in a society of closed minds, vacant ears and a cold heart. The idea is to inspire by giving new life through an old medium.

Hustle Poet Vol I will be the first book in a poetry anthology due out in 2021.

To her credit, Amaarah has penned:
The Vaughan Chronicles: Magnolia Like the Flower (2012)

The Vaughan Chronicles: Burning Blossom (2015)
The Vaughan Chronicles: Starshine (2016)
The Silent Violent Few (2014)
The Silent Violent Few: Risen (2015)
The Silent Violent Few: Noir (2016)
Chariot of Constance (2016)
The Monster Inside (2018)
The Cathedral Saga: The Receiver (2017)
The Cathedral Saga: Reign (2021)
Scissorwood Drive (Est. Release 2022)
The Jarred Heart of Amara Grace (Est. Release Late 2022)
Hustle Poet Vol. I: The Beginning will be the first book in a
poetry anthology due out in 2021.
Hustle Poet: Vol II: The Continuation (March 2022)
Hustle Poet: Vol III: The Current Situation (November
2022)
 Toxic City: Opera Omina Vol. I (October 2021)
Toxic City: Opera Omina Vol. II (April 2022)

Amaarah is the Creator/Producer behind:
In The Pod with Hustle Poet Podcast (2020/2021/2022)
Toxic City: Opera Omina (2021/2022)
Stories from the Pod: (2021/2022)

All podcasts are available on iHeartRadio, Spotify, Audible,
Stitcher & Amazon Music.

CPSIA information can be obtained
at www.ICGtesting.com
Printed in the USA
LVRC091952101121
702999LV00004B/14